sling shot

Andrew Ogun

LUCENT DREAMING

First Edition

Slingshot
Published by Lucent Dreaming Ltd.
103 Bute Street, Cardiff, CF10 5AD

Copyright © 2024 Andrew Ogun
All rights reserved. Printed in the United Kingdom by 4edge.
No part of this book may be reproduced without written permission
from the author.

Andrew Ogun has asserted the author's right under the Copyright,
Designs and Patents Act 1988 to be identified as author of this work.

Cover illustration © 2024 Regan Giflin

ISBN 978-1-7396609-5-6

Lucent Dreaming acknowledges the financial support of
Books Council of Wales and Creative Wales.

To my younger self.

All that confusion, restlessness, curiosity, anguish, self-loathing, shame, precociousness, dissatisfaction, insomnia, hunger, passion, blind faith, questioning and belief in something greater was not in vain.

Every moment, the good, the bad and the ugly, led to this body of work. You did it. I hope this gives you even a little bit of the peace and contentment you continue to search and fight for.

Content Warning:

This collection contains references to suicidal ideation from the start.

Contents

Suicide Note	11
The Gift	13
Someone Was Here	14
Where Does It All Go?	15
Shadow Self	16
Man vs Self	17
The Score	18
Ego Death	19
Shedding Skin	20
Quicksand	21
Delayed Gratification	22
Touching Distance	23
The Search	24
Of Kings and Men	25
Sins of the Father	26
The Perfect Man	28
Somersaults	29
Andrea	30
Andrew	32
Arafat	33
Ogun	34
Ojapiano	35
Dust	36
A Zoom Burial	37

Message in a Bottle	38
We Walk with Them	39
A Seat at the Table	40
Dreamachine	42
Bad Business	44
A-Side	46
B-Side	47
The Heretic	48
The Cycle Continues	50
Slingshot	51

Slingshot   9

Suicide Note

I told my therapist the other day about
The night in Rotterdam when I almost
Killed myself, how beautiful and alluring
The water looked, how the water was
Calling me, calling me like the sound of
An early morning prayer,
I was close to being enchanted
By the beauty of it all,
By the prospect of eternal peace,
By the prospect of being the master
Of my own destiny
And my own demise.

He asked me to give him a percentage
Of how close I was and I said seventy.
The only thing that anchored me
Was the thought of my sister.
She's twelve now, old enough to remember me
And all the moments that we had.
How would she react if they told her that
Her brother decided to kill himself in Rotterdam?
So after staring into the nothingness
Itching to hit the water,
Pleading with the waves to wash away
This curse of consciousness,
I put on my straitjacket and
Walked back to the hotel.

What triggered this, he asked.
Nothing, I had a great day in fact.
He stopped me there and reiterated
Something he'd said before about
People who have always been in
Fight or flight –
They don't know what to do in the
Absence of chaos.

I told him that it's just like Chekhov's Gun
And I'm not really sure what Act we're now on.
The gun remains on the wall,
Untouched for the time being
But still omniscient, omnipotent, omnipresent.

The Gift

'Less morose and more present' — *Rostam Batmanglij*

I am here.
In this moment.
On this page.
On this planet.

Someone Was Here

A beheaded Buddha sits atop a pile of books –
*The Weary Sons of Freud, Meditations in an Emergency,
Crime and Punishment*
A part of the whole, a snapshot in time,
A marker of the man that once lived there,
His scent, opaque, distinct, still lingers,
His fragments come alive if you get too close,
The air,
Heavy and unforgiving.

He no longer resides here.
Perhaps he never did
In any tangible, material way
But his spirit remains –
Weaved into the books,
The paintings,
The clothes,
The rug,
The lamp,
The plants,
Even the room itself.

Where Does It All Go?

Where does it all go?
Does it go up in the air with the fumes of the chain smoke
Or does it go down with the ship like the captain?
Maybe it goes wherever I go
Like the sun when I was little
Or maybe it walks in front
Like a protective parent.
Where does it all go?
I asked my mother but she didn't know
I asked my father but he never answers
I asked the heavens but they stayed silent
I thought about asking you
But you probably don't know either
So I asked myself,
Where does it all go?
It goes where things go to die
And are reborn
It goes where you reap what you sow
And sow what you reap
Right into the belly of the beast
Where the sombre meet
To host seances and have siestas
To speak with those that can
Tell us where it all goes.

Shadow Self

That figure at the end of my bed
Could be friend or could be foe,
Who wants to know?
It appears like a fever dream,
The grimmest of reapers,
Dressed like a funeral,
Smile like *A Portrait of the Artist as a Shadow of His Former Self,*
A blackened body that is obscure yet familiar,
A sleek shadow formed in the fog of incense,
Its face lit only by a cut-price candlelight.

It invites me to step
Into the shadows,
Into the depths of a darkness
Deeper than the unmarred parts of an ocean
As I sink into a half-wake, half-sleep state
Still wondering,
Is this a warm embrace
Or the bittersweet taste of a hangover
From a past life?

Man vs Self

'At war with myself, I only spar with the greatest' — Cee Major

Wars are not just fought on the frontlines
They're fought in the trenches of your mind
In the nooks and the crannies
In the blind spots
Where all is dark
And the only light
Is the sight of limbs
And all that's heard
Are the screams
Of other fighters
But you can't hear it because
The shots are too loud
And the blood is too red
Making you realise that there is a
War on Terror
War on Drugs
What about the War on Us?

The Score

The body keeps the score even when
The mind tries to play tricks like déjà vu
There is no grand finale, no fanfare, no signal
Just a body that keeps the score
And a mind that tries to play tricks like
A con artist on his last dime but little
Does the mind know that the body keeps
The score and whilst men lie, women lie
And children lie, the body doesn't
And right now the score is

Ego Death

For the ego to be reborn
It first must die and
It must die a violent death
Hung, drawn and quartered
Or brought before the guillotine
Not in its sleep
Not of old age
Not due to sickness
That will not suffice.

The Firing Squad is my preferred method
Shot at dawn
Right before the first light
Just before the first cigarette of the day
As the darkness slithers away
And the sky looks bathed in grey
Shots ringing in the air like the Battle of Marseille.

You wanna see a dead body?
Is what the kids will say when one
Stumbles across this ego on the railway
Not knowing that the same fate awaits
All those that dare to be great.

Shedding Skin

I scratch at the skin I've been in for
Far longer than I care to remember
Layer after layer
Piece by piece
It begins to shed
Marred and macabre
Bruised and battered
Unrecognisable to the naked eye.

It peels like paint
It feels like fingernails on a chalkboard
And it lasts a lifetime
The skin loosens and tightens
Falls and forms
Fights to cling on to its wearer.

I twist and turn
Trying to shed the skin I've been in for
Far longer than I care to remember but
This skin is stubborn like an old soul
And it just won't let go
Like a new-born holding on to all it knows
And all it ever will know.

Quicksand

I stand with my feet pressed firmly on the ground
If only they knew that I am stood in quicksand
Sinking into an abyss of dismembered hands
Hands that belonged to the men, women and children
Who sank before me.

Delayed Gratification

I pray that one day someone will teach me
The art of delay.
It's supposed to be *each one, teach one*
So why have you left me in the lurch?
Flights can, Transport for Wales can
So why can't I do it too?

The politicians keep telling me to do it
My mother keeps telling me to do it
But I can't seem to get the hang of it
And if I don't get the hang of *it*
The hangman will get the hang of *me*
And that would be a tragedy
Of a Greek kind
Without any of the humour
Maybe there will be a catharsis
And a standing ovation too
If not for me then maybe for you.

Touching Distance

Maybe you get closer and closer
To touching it with every life lived
In glimpses and flashes
Small miracle by small miracle
Like every stone skipped
On never-ending waters
Like every glass clinked
In rooms never gleaned
And moments never seen
Like every whisper that fills
The space between you and me,
An arm's length, touching distance
But just out of reach, even at
Full stretch

The Search

You walk up and down this world aimlessly
Chasing one cheap thrill after another
Hungry, hollow, but hopeful.

A mouthful is never enough to curb the appetite
Like watering a bucket with a hole at the bottom
But the bottom isn't quite so bad
It's cosy down there
I've been there before
I can see you have too
Just remember this house is not a home
You will find what you are looking for
In this life or the next.

Of Kings and Men

When one has lived like a King
You don't mourn or grieve when they're gone.
You stay steady, you steady the ship
And you steady the seas
And you drink yourself silly
In celebration of a life fully lived,
A life fully conquered.

When one has lived like a King
You don't mourn or grieve when they're gone.
You stay steady, you dust off your armour
And you raise your sword
In the air for a man who died
Exactly how he lived.

When one has lived like a King
The only thing he craves is the life
Of the common man,
For what he could not reach whilst
He was reigning, he can only hope
To reach as he is rotting.

Sins of the Father

The sins of the father do not disappear
They do not get written off
You are required to pay the debt in full
No payment plans
No subsidies
No sympathy
One lump sum
No credit
No debit
No change given.

The sins of the father do not disappear
They do not get written off
You are required to pay the debt in blood
No cooling off
No guarantor
No pity
One whole payment
No Apple Pay
No delay
Exact change only.

The sins of the father do not disappear
They do not get written off
You are required to pay the debt in death
No government debt relief
No charities
No mercy
Straight cash

No cheques
No sex
Notes not accepted.

The sins of the father do not disappear
They do not get written off
They accumulate with time
They feed on soul after soul
They feast on the pockets of the innocent
And flourish on the depths of your despair
Until you are just a *Ghost in the Shell*
Wearing the sins of your father like a cheap suit
Carrying the sins of your father like a talisman.

The Perfect Man

I ain't no perfect man, I'm tryna do the best that I can with what it is I have
— Mos Def

Sometimes I wish I was the Perfect Man,
Not for me, just for you,
For the sake of all your wishes coming true
For the sake of all your visions old and new
For the sake of all your deepest blues
For the sake of all that you've been through.

Somersaults

Mother's incessant warnings
Are no match for your zest and the
Fine margins between glee and paralysis
Put an extra spring in your step
And an extra bounce on the trampoline.

Like a coin you flip and you flip and you flip
Not knowing whether it will be heads or tails,
Heaven or Hell or Olympic gold,
Getting closer to the Sun,
Hoping you don't share the same fate
As Icarus, as the watchful eye
Of Daedalus keeps you in check.

Forwards and backwards
Backwards and forwards
Moving from one part of the
Trampoline to the next like destiny,
And you may not be able to reach
The sky today but it will not deter you
From trying again tomorrow despite
Mother's incessant warnings.

Andrea

Against the backdrop of Lago di Como
A Black Swan was brought into the world
With the help of Sicilian generosity
And Nigerian resilience.

Born in silence, awoken by a slap to the cheek,
The boy's cry marked a new beginning.
He was named after his Godfather
Not the movie but the man who was the
Closest thing he ever had to a father because
Like so many others, his father was just
Snippets and stories with no flesh, no bones
And no soul.

Whilst his mother was out doing what she had to do
To put food on the table, the boy was raised
In a home of love and kindness
That knew no bounds and had no limits.
The English words that he bends to his will
Today did not exist back then,
Only Sicilian slang and an Italian twang
That has faded into a painful memory
And frustrated, disconnected conversations
Fuelled by nothing except an everlasting love.

Parlava un italiano perfetto, cosa
È successo? His Godmother would say,
Not knowing that the sabre-tooth of assimilation
Annihilated everything that he knew,
Annihilated every ounce of comfort.

Now *Andrea* is a name that is only said
In the confines of spaces
That few are privy to.

Andrew

It doesn't have the instant appeal of
Andrea or the power of Ogun or
The mysticism of Arafat.

It's a Plain Jane, a reminder of
The Black Hole of anglicisation
And a lifetime of mispronounced names.
You don't look like an *Andrew*
They used to tell me
That's because I was not an *Andrew*
But my tongue became tied and I began to wear
The name like a hand-me-down
That is a tad too big.
The other kids would say their names
Like a badge of honour,
I would say my name as if I had
A frog stuck in my throat.

I had to become *Andrew* to become British,
To move from the caste of the second-class citizen
To the caste of those who could lock eyes
And shake hands with anyone they pleased,
To be able to move with an ease
That comes with belonging,
An ease that eludes the Other and
Shrouds the murkiness beneath it all
And what is the point of it all?
The all that is underneath the surface?
The all that imbues that sense of power in a name?

Arafat

A name that holds no weight like the paper planes
Of juvenile schoolboys
Uttered only by you or uttered in jest
By us but somehow I still shudder
Every time I read the name *Arafat*
On the odd occasions when you text me.
Rather than mercy it is callousness that comes to
Mind when I think of that name
There will be no pilgrimages today
There will be no grand speeches on the
Mount where the Prophet himself stood.
The name sits somewhere in my limbic system
Existing only in fruitless attempts
To make a connection that will never be made
And jokes that barely mask the pangs of the pain.

Ogun

Warrior.
The one who opens the way.
God of all things iron.
Essence of destruction and creativity.
Artist.
Anchored.
Boundless.
A symbol of resistance.
A symbol of pride.
A symbol of sacrifice.
A tale for the grandkids.
The beginning of infinity.
The pressure of legacy.
Trials and triumphs.
Embodiment of the struggle.
Heavy weight on its shoulders.
Noose on its neck.

Ojapiano

My cousin told me a story about a
Boy in the village who plays the flute.

In the story, the Boy plays the flute
So well because his spirit is the one
Actually playing and all the Native Doctors
In Nigeria call on him when they want to
Call to the dead
So the Boy plays with everything he has
Moving from the physical to the spiritual
Enchanting or bewitching
Anyone who dares to listen.

He has no name
All he has is his flute.

Dust

I will not turn to dust in foreign lands.

Though my heart beats to the drum of
Eurocentricity, Renaissance Art and Reality Television,
I will not turn to dust in foreign lands.

Even when I demonstrate my standard, British charm
And sing *You'll Never Walk Alone* with goosebumps on my arms,
I will not turn to dust in foreign lands.

I may have some pub grub from time to time,
Shepherd's pie, gammon, egg and chips or just a pint,
I will not turn to dust in foreign lands.

As I become wiser and my hands become wizened,
I see the sun-tinged lands of my forefathers on the horizon,
I see carefree children, guarding the waves like Poseidon,
I see elders, tribesmen, chiefs and Mayans.
I drink from the fountains of mythology and legends,
The juju in the air makes me pause for a second,
Black Skin, White Masks, can you feel the tension?

Ashes to ashes, dust to dust,
Why do these foreign lands
Expect me to adjust?
I dance to the rhythm of my own drums,
I dance to the rhythm because it's a must
And as soon as I'm home, I'm sure I'll turn to dust.

A Zoom Burial

Your body is enshrined in linen so white
That it makes the waves of the sea look lifeless.
Facing Mecca, from where you come you must return
Even though I shiver at the thought
Of your linen-clad body lying there without
Anybody or anything.

How I long to touch the soil that you lay on,
How I long to join them all in prayer
But this longing cannot be satisfied
And I am forced to be soothed by
The virtual offerings of Zoom.

Message in a Bottle

I found a message in a bottle today, it made me think of you,
I watched it wash ashore whilst I was waiting for Godot
But he never came and neither did you.

We Walk with Them

We walk with them everywhere we go,
One foot in front of the other,
Bare feet on the solid ground,
Incensed murmurs floating through
The air as we walk with them,
Shoulder to shoulder,
Carrying the annals of our ancestors
Everywhere we go,
Walking alongside the Mystics
Of the past, praising Jah, Oshun, Olokun
Or anyone that will listen,
Seeing through the eyes of those
That came before us and those
That will come after us,
Sending our blessings
To the highest of highs,
The mountains after the mountain,
The moment after the moment,
Heart beating to that ancient drum,
That feverish sound,
As we walk and we walk and we walk
And we walk

A Seat at the Table

There was once a version of us that was
Content with a seat at the table,
A table that has us playing musical chairs
For our entire lives, sitting us next to people
Who would rather be sat next to ghosts than us,
Placing us in seats that never allow us to be still.

We imagine futures with flying cars,
Microchips and life on the moon.
I imagine a future with space,
Space cultivated by us, for us,
Space that gives wings to communities,
Space overflowing with creative expression,
Space filled to the brim with joy.

We imagine futures with floating cities,
Robots and life on Mars.
I imagine a future that takes us back to our root,
A root that is grounded yet elevated,
A root that bends yet never breaks,
A root with no centre and no borders,
A root with no beginning, middle or ending.

Today, we smile whilst we suffer.
Tomorrow, we smile whilst we prosper.
The future belongs to our Afros,
Our Agbadas, our Niqabs
And our Burqas.

How long have we been dancing to
The beat of drums that can never capture
The rhythm of our hearts, our heritage and our histories?
The drums that we dance to today will become
An echo to the drums that we will dance to tomorrow,
The tables will turn, our feet will be blackened
As we groove from sunrise to sundown
To a sound only we can pronounce.

Dreamachine

Shades of blue unseen and unknown
With no synonym or antonym
No origin or final destination
Yet I find myself here
Not in flesh but in spirit
Anticipating, waiting,
As if I know what to expect
But I cannot know what to expect
Because I'm only a mortal man
And this is a place reserved for those
Who are not normally found here.

Step into the Dreamachine says the voice
On the tannoy *1984*-like and I can feel
The Ghost of Orwell slinking through the system
The Ghost is trying to tell me something but
The message gets lost in transmission and
All I can think about is how cold it is in here.

Step into the Dreamachine says the voice
On the tannoy only this time it's more like
A Clockwork Orange but The Ghost of Burgess
Did not appear although the message got through
Loud and clear so I step,
I step like an infant who has just discovered
The wonders of the world
I close my eyes and I'm greeted by a mirage
But it is not water that I see
Rather everything and nothing at all

And the shades of blue remain etched
In my mind's eye as a reminder that
The Dreamachine is here to stay.

Bad Business

Everyone is hiding behind tinted glasses
To cover the dead behind their eyes.
There's nothing but bad business here
But we barter and banter as the beer flows
Tucked under the glow of streetlights
Shrouded by a smog the locals never
Seem to get lost in.

The visitors struggle to acclimatise but
Whenever they ask questions they're told
That magicians never reveal their tricks
And are left alone to navigate the mist
Amidst the hustle and bustle of this place full of
Slicks
The poor
The rich
The glam
The glitz
And everyone else looking for a quick fix.

All are welcome here.
The only rule is that you play possum
Or you'll end up as prey
Can't let them know there's still blood
Coursing in those veins
Don't want to end up as a trophy on display
So you're forced to play the game
Making backstreet deals in narrow alleyways
With predators that would have you for lunch

Mingling amongst thieves that have no honour
But will drink with you all day, everyday
Pokerfaced telling you to speak up
If you have something to say.

A-Side

Off the A-Side
Record spinning as I spin with it
How many beats per minute?
Enough to come out of my chest
Your heart don't stand a chance is what
Anderson Paak said
Now I know what he meant
Just let that Jazz play until day breaks
Serenade me with the sweet synaesthesia
Seeping through the speakers
Transporting me to a time probably
Quite similar to mine
Where rhythm and rhyme
Were signs of The Sublime
Line by line
Chorus after chorus
I am taken to a place beyond borders
Where there is no Other and no order.

B-Side

Some say the B-side is better
Less commercial
More human
The comedown after the come up
A chopped and screwed kaleidoscope
After the slow rush
DHL on repeat
Stood up because the room has no seats
Framed fragments of the beat
Hallucinations of the music sheet
Notes upon notes
A myriad of hope
A slippery slope
A crutch used to cope
Hardly sleep, faith was in the coffee bean is what
Frank Ocean said
Now I know what he meant.

The Heretic

When you look up at the sky
And hear the birds singing
Or the rain pouring
Or the sun shining,
You have no doubts
How can you?
When the birds are serenading you
And the rain greets you
And the Sun smiles at you as if
You were her own son.

When you look into the eyes of someone
You love and you see flames,
Flames of rage or flames of passion,
You still have no doubts,
How could you?
That would make you either a fool or a heretic.

But the birds are not always singing,
Sometimes they decide to
Take their vows and as you look up
To the sky hoping to hear that
Sweet, sweet melody one more time,
You are only met by the
Sound of sleep, and although you want
The rain to be pleasant it is violent
And as you look up at the sky in anticipation
For the rain to nourish you,
You are only met by the fury

And power of Mother Nature,
And sometimes although the clouds seem to
Welcome you with open arms
And step aside for the Sun
To be the star of the show,
You are only met by her solemnity,
And a frown awaits you,
No smiles today.

When I stare into the eyes of humanity,
All I see and all I feel is doubt,
As we plummet towards oblivion
And ignorance wears the world's
Most decorated crown,
All I feel is doubt because if there is
Somebody home
They refuse to open the door
And for some reason,
They won't check the window.

The Cycle Continues

Have you ever watched a flower
That you carefully cultivated
Wilt before your very eyes?
Minimal external influence
Maximum attention paid
But still the flower decays
And you remain powerless to
Prevent the inevitable.

This flower -
This extension of you,
Your hopes
Your dreams
Your fears
Your nightmares
Your cynicism
Your optimism,
Corrupted almost beyond recognition
And thus the cycle continues,
The trauma chain remains unbroken,
The generational curses persist,
And the burden of cultivating a
Flower that will flourish in the
Harshest of conditions passes from
One person to the next.

Slingshot

A slingshot in the hands of the right person
Can topple tyrants, end empires and
Make martyrs of men,
Allowing you to right revolutionary wrongs
And reach heights you may have only dreamed of
Or read about in fictions and fables
Or tall tales the Olders would tell you
But they only mention the stories of glory.

The dance between you and I
Is one of desire and destination,
The here and now
And a tomorrow that is never promised
But comes closer and closer
As you pull back, praying,
That you do not become just another
Cog in our cruel machine,
Another footnote in a book
That nobody reads,
A mouth that nobody ever feeds,
Just a speck of blood on the leaves,
One eye closed,
The wink before the release.

We ride on the winds, wherever they blow,
Hoping to reach our target before
We become hidden histories that are
Never wrote, only told in passing

As a rite of passage
So the next David
Can slay Goliath,
Chest high, stood defiant,
A stone's throw away
From making a mark
And marking the moment,
My moment.

Acknowledgements

I am forever indebted to so many people and so many things that words could never do it justice. I must start with thanking my mother. The magnitude of your strength and your sacrifices are boundless, and I hope you know how grateful I am for everything you have done and continue to do for me. You are a beacon of all things good in this world.

To Brandy and Brenda, my Northern Stars, my heartbeat, the reason why I wake up in the morning and try to be a better man and a better human. You both give me a sense of purpose. You are both the anchors of my life, and for you both I would lay down my life at any moment without hesitation.

To Faith, my mini me, Lil Ogun, it has been my pleasure to see you grow and flourish into the person you are today. Life will continue to try and throw you off course, but I will always be there to help get you back on track. Keep being you, your potential is limitless and don't let anyone tell you otherwise.

To Jannat, I simply cannot thank you enough. Without you, there is no *Slingshot*. You took a chance on me barely knowing me or my work, and I hope that I can repay the faith you showed in me. I have made a friend for life in you from this process.

Your empathy, warmth and considerate nature is what enabled me to express myself in the way that I have throughout this collection and in our conversations. I don't even know if I ever will be able to repay you but I'll never stop trying. You have pushed me to become a much better poet and more importantly, a much better person.

To my therapist, I don't know how much I can say but thank you. Seriously, thank you.

To all the people that read the collection and gave their feedback and perspective, thank you all for caring enough to allow me to share my world with you. Care is a precious commodity, and so is time, so I do not take it for granted that you gave me both. Call on me whenever you need and I assure you I will be there.

To all the experiences, stories, conversations and people that inspired *Slingshot*, you are the catalysts for everything that can be found in this collection. Without you, there is no work and there is no life. The only thing the artist can hope for is that we do justice to the things that inspire us, stir us and move us.

And lastly, to you, the reader. I hope something touches your heart within this collection. I hope these words make you feel something, whatever that feeling is. I went to places I have never been before to write this work and I am grateful to have you on the journey.

About the Author

Andrew Ogun is a musician, poet, creative director and activist from Newport. He is the main organiser for BLM Gwent and is also the Agent for Change at the Arts Council of Wales. His work is centred on identity and capturing the tensions of the human experience.